PIANO • VOCAL • GUITAR

THE SONGS
IRVING BERLIN
MOVIE SONGS

Irving Berlin logo and Irving Berlin Music Company are registered trademarks of the Estate of Irving Berlin.

Cover Photo: Irving Berlin in Hollywood, circa mid-1930's.

ISBN 0-7935-0379-5

 Hal Leonard Publishing Corporation

7777 West Bluemound Road P.O. Box 13819 Milwaukee, WI 53213

Irving Berlin, Judy Garland, Fred Astaire

THE SONGS OF
IRVING BERLIN
MOVIE SONGS

CONTENTS

4 Be Careful, It's My Heart *1942*
HOLIDAY INN

12 Best Things Happen While
You're Dancing, The *1953*
WHITE CHRISTMAS

8 Better Luck Next Time *1947*
EASTER PARADE

18 Change Partners *1938*
CAREFREE

22 Cheek To Cheek *1935*
TOP HAT

28 Couple Of Swells, A *1947*
EASTER PARADE

32 Easter Parade *1933*
EASTER PARADE *1948*

15 Happy Holiday *1942*
HOLIDAY INN

36 I Used To Be Color Blind *1938*
CAREFREE

40 I'd Rather Lead A Band *1936*
FOLLOW THE FLEET

50 I'm Putting All My Eggs In One Basket *1936*
FOLLOW THE FLEET

45 Isn't This A Lovely Day
(To Be Caught In The Rain?) *1935*
TOP HAT

54 It Only Happens When I Dance With You *1947*
EASTER PARADE

60 Let Yourself Go *1936*
FOLLOW THE FLEET

64 Let's Face The Music And Dance *1936*
FOLLOW THE FLEET

57 Let's Start The New Year Right *1942*
HOLIDAY INN

68 Love, You Didn't Do Right By Me *1953*
WHITE CHRISTMAS

78 No Strings (I'm Fancy Free) *1935*
TOP HAT

82 Now It Can Be Told *1938*
ALEXANDER'S RAGTIME BAND

71 Piccolino, The *1935*
TOP HAT

86 Plenty To Be Thankful For *1942*
HOLIDAY INN

90 Sisters *1953*
WHITE CHRISTMAS

94 Steppin' Out With My Baby *1947*
EASTER PARADE

98 This Year's Kisses *1937*
ON THE AVENUE

102 Top Hat, White Tie And Tails *1935*
TOP HAT

107 When Winter Comes *1939*
SECOND FIDDLE

112 White Christmas *1942*
HOLIDAY INN

116 You Keep Coming Back Like A Song *1943*
BLUE SKIES

124 You're Easy To Dance With *1942*
HOLIDAY INN

120 You're Laughing At Me *1937*
ON THE AVENUE

BE CAREFUL, IT'S MY HEART

Words and Music by
IRVING BERLIN

BETTER LUCK NEXT TIME

Words and Music by
IRVING BERLIN

For ev - 'ry rose that with - ers and dies, an -

oth - er blooms in its stead. A new love waits to

o - pen its eyes af - ter the old love is dead. That

THE BEST THINGS HAPPEN WHILE YOU'RE DANCING

Words and Music by
IRVING BERLIN

HAPPY HOLIDAY

Words and Music by
IRVING BERLIN

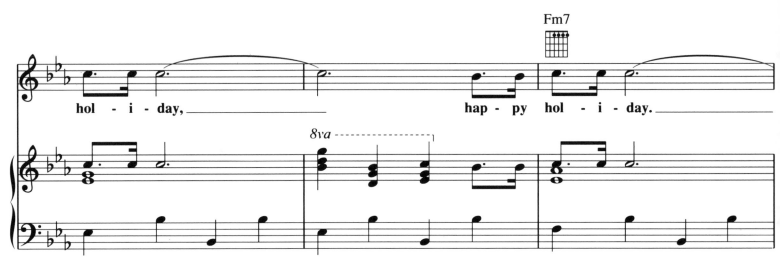

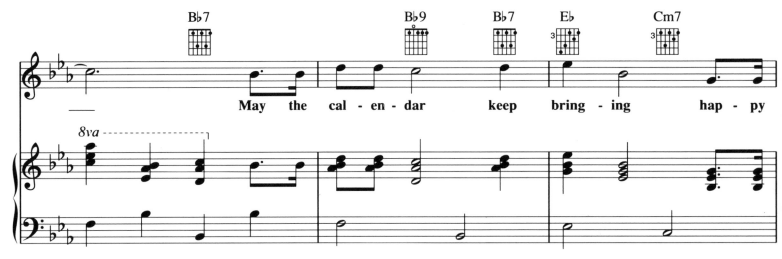

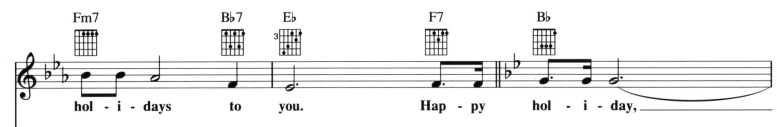

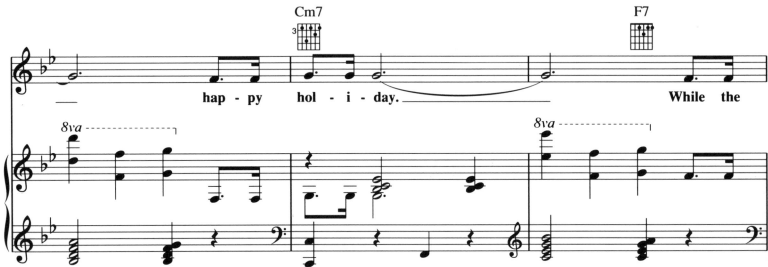

CHANGE PARTNERS

Words and Music by
IRVING BERLIN

CHEEK TO CHEEK

Words and Music by
IRVING BERLIN

Heav - en, _____ I'm in Heav - en.

And my heart beats so that I can hard - ly speak. _____

A COUPLE OF SWELLS

Words and Music by
IRVING BERLIN

We're a cou-ple of swells; we stop at the best ho-
Wall Street Bank-ers are we, with plen-ty of cur-ren-

tels. But we pre-fer the coun-try far a-
cy. We'd o-pen up the safe, but we for-

way from the cit-y smells.
got where we put the key.

EASTER PARADE

Words and Music by
IRVING BERLIN

I USED TO BE COLOR BLIND

Words and Music by
IRVING BERLIN

I'D RATHER LEAD A BAND

Words and Music by
IRVING BERLIN

Moderately

Lyrics:
I have - n't am - bi - tions
for lof - ty po - si - tions that wind up with the wealth _ of the
land. I'd give _ you the throne that _ a king sat _ on

ISN'T THIS A LOVELY DAY
(TO BE CAUGHT IN THE RAIN?)

Words and Music by
IRVING BERLIN

Slow Swing

Lyrics:
The weath-er is fright-'ning, the thun-der and light-'ning seem to be hav-ing their way. But as far as I'm con-cerned, it's a love-ly day. The

I'M PUTTING ALL MY EGGS
IN ONE BASKET

Words and Music by
IRVING BERLIN

52

IT ONLY HAPPENS WHEN
I DANCE WITH YOU

Words and Music by
IRVING BERLIN

LET'S START THE NEW YEAR RIGHT

Words and Music by
IRVING BERLIN

One min-ute to mid-night, one min-ute to go.

One min-ute to say "good-bye" be-fore we say "hel-

lo." Let's start the New Year right, ___ twelve o'-

LET YOURSELF GO

Words and Music by
IRVING BERLIN

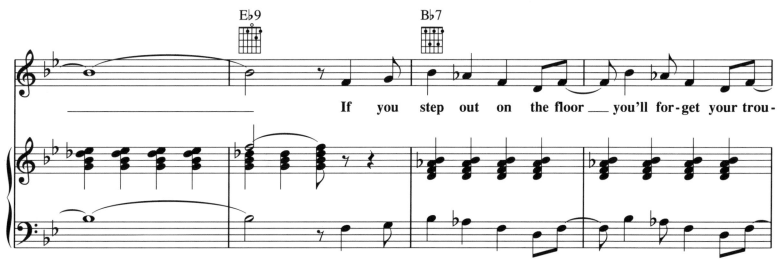

If you step out on the floor ___ you'll for-get your trou-

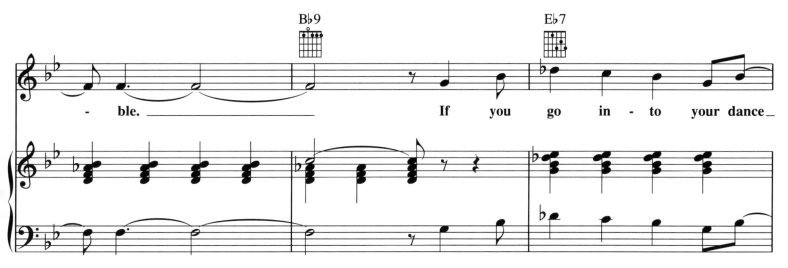

-ble. ___ If you go in-to your dance ___

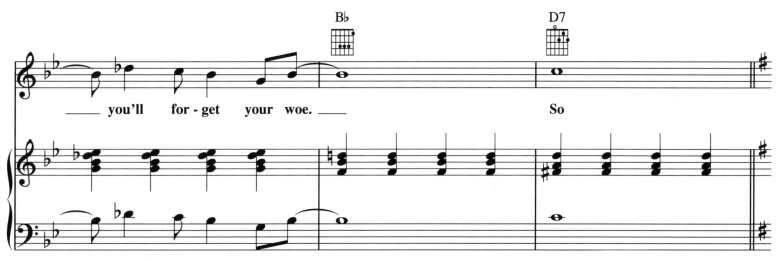

___ you'll for-get your woe. ___ So

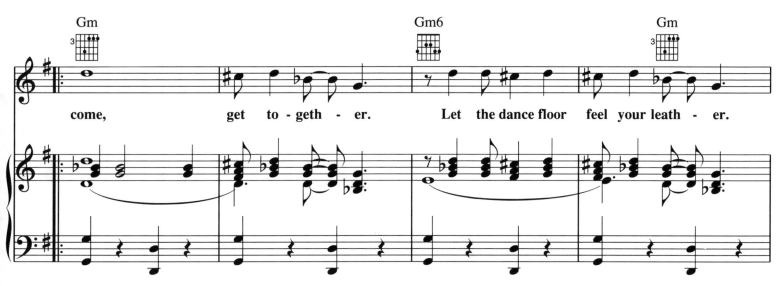

come, get to-geth-er. Let the dance floor feel your leath-er.

Step as light-ly as a feath-er. Let ___ your-self go. ___

Come hit the tim-ber. Loos-en up and start to lim-ber.

Can't you hear that hot ma-rim-ba? Let ___ your-self go. ___

Let your-self go, ___ re-lax, and let your-self go. ___ Re-lax, you've

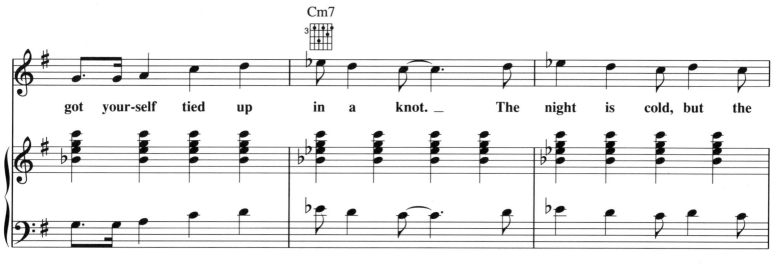

got your-self tied up in a knot. ___ The night is cold, but the

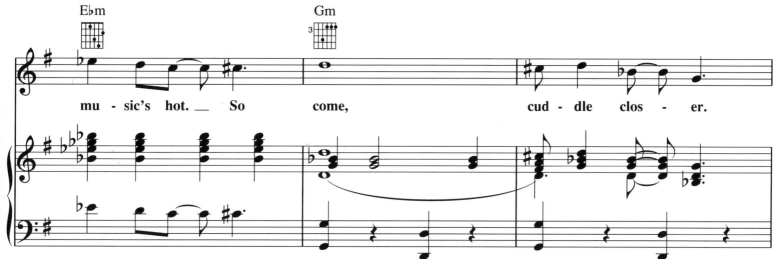

mu - sic's hot. ___ So come, cud - dle clos - er.

Don't you dare to an - swer, "No ___ Sir." Butch - er, bank - er,

clerk and gro - cer, let ___ your-self go. ___

LET'S FACE THE MUSIC AND DANCE

Words and Music by
IRVING BERLIN

LOVE, YOU DIDN'T DO RIGHT BY ME

Words and Music by
IRVING BERLIN

Love, _____ you did-n't do right by me.

You planned a ro-mance that just had-n't a chance and I'm through. _____

Love,

THE PICCOLINO

Words and Music by
IRVING BERLIN

NO STRINGS (I'M FANCY FREE)

Words and Music by
IRVING BERLIN

NOW IT CAN BE TOLD

Words and Music by
IRVING BERLIN

All the world's great lov-ers have been glo-ri-fied.

Hist-'ry placed them in a ro-man-tic set.

In be-tween book cov-ers they are side by side.

PLENTY TO BE THANKFUL FOR

Words and Music by
IRVING BERLIN

SISTERS

Words and Music by
IRVING BERLIN

Sis - ters,   sis - ters,
(Male) Broth - ers,   broth - ers,

there were nev - er such de - vot - ed sis - ters.   Nev - er had to have a chap - er-
there were nev - er such de - vot - ed broth - ers.   When there comes a glam - our girl who's

STEPPIN' OUT WITH MY BABY

Words and Music by
IRVING BERLIN

Lyrics:
If I seem to scin-til-late___ it's be-cause I've got a date, ___

a date with a pack-age of___ the good things that

come with love. ___ You don't have to ask me, ___

THIS YEAR'S KISSES

Words and Music by
IRVING BERLIN

TOP HAT, WHITE TIE AND TAILS

Words and Music by
IRVING BERLIN

WHEN WINTER COMES

Words and Music by
IRVING BERLIN

WHITE CHRISTMAS

Words and Music by
IRVING BERLIN

YOU KEEP COMING BACK LIKE A SONG

Words and Music by
IRVING BERLIN

YOU'RE LAUGHING AT ME

Words and Music by
IRVING BERLIN

YOU'RE EASY TO DANCE WITH

Words and Music by
IRVING BERLIN